Rocks a

Content

About this unit

This unit introduces children to the idea that the Earth is made up of rock – even if they can't always see it. The children learn that rocks break down into pebbles and soil. Children also learn the difference between some rocks and between soils and discover their different uses. Children begin to use the vocabulary related to rocks and soils, introducing the names of familiar rocks such as marble, clay and chalk.

Scientific enquiry is planned into the unit and focuses on:

- measuring time and measuring amounts of liquid.
- planning a fair test.
- applying knowledge gained from observations and enquiries.
- collecting evidence and recognising and avoiding hazards and risks.

Background Scientific Information

We live on a rocky planet. Wherever we are, even in the middle of the ocean, there are rocks beneath our feet. These rocks were formed as the Earth began to cool. The cooling process is far from over. Under the hard, cold crust, the mantle and core of the planet are still intensely hot – so hot that molten rock periodically bursts through volcanoes.

Much of the rock on the Earth's surface was formed from the original molten material, this is called **igneous** rock. Other types of rock have been eroded, transported and laid down in layers of sediment - the **sedimentary** rocks. Some have been subjected to intense heat and pressure and have changed or metamorphosed over time – the **metamorphic** rocks. We take these rocks and their products for granted. They are all around us. We use marble or granite for building and slate for roofs. Rock is heavy stuff to cart about, and so buildings often reflect the local materials available in the area.

The weather transforms rocks. Even the strongest rock can be split by the 'ice wedge' – water entering cracks in the rock, freezing, expanding and splitting the rock apart. Smaller rocks are acted on by wind and rain, by the sea or by plant or animal action. Finally they break down to tiny particles which, mixed with organic matter from plants or animals, makes up soil.

Soil is important for plant growth, and plant roots are important for securing the soil against erosion and weathering. When the soil is made of very fine particles that can be suspended in water, we say that the soil is **clay**. Where the particles are fairly large and can be poured, we say that the soil is **sandy**. Most soils are somewhere between these two. **Loam** is a mixture of clay and sand and offers a good balance of drainage, security and nutrients to growing plants.

The study of rocks and soils at primary school is mostly concerned with the recognition of rock types (slate, marble, chalk, granite, sand or clay), and with the different forms of rocks (pebbles, stones). It also explores the characteristics of rocks and soils – their colour, texture, drainage and absorbency, and what they are used for in the world around us.

For example, clay is used to make pottery and tiles, and sand mixed with other rock ingredients is used to make cement and concrete. The Earth's crust also contains metal ores, which are refined to make various familiar objects. The recent discovery of ways to change the chemical structure of oils has led to the petro-chemical industry and the development of plastics. The petro-chemical industry depends on fossil fuels embedded in rock. Plant fossils and the fossils of marine life are two important fossil energy sources. Burning them may be contributing to global warming.

Information and Communication Technology

Where appropriate, ideas for ICT opportunities are included throughout the Teacher's Notes. The table below indicates where ICT skills could be developed in this unit.

Task number	ICT Opportunity
1 Rocks and soils in the kitchen	*Research materials that originate from rocks using CD-ROMs or Internet.*
2 How are they different?	*Research the origins of rock using CD-ROMs or Internet.*
4 How hard?	*Use computer software to record findings on the properties of rocks.*
5 Scratch test	*Use computer software to store information and classify rocks.*
8 Where does soil come from?	*Use a simple graphics programme to illustrate how rocks become soil.*
12 Which soils drain the fastest?	*Record findings on a database and create a graph using computer software.*
14 Hannah's test	*Create a graph using computer software.*

Scheme of Work:

Learning objective: Knowledge and understanding	Task	Learning objective: Skills	Literacy and numeracy links	Resources and safety	Evidence of learning Children:
To understand that rocks are used for a variety of everyday purposes.	**1 Rocks and soils in the kitchen.** Children learn to recognise materials that have originated from rocks.			**Task Sheet 1.** CD-ROMs and Internet.	Can identify uses of rocks and soils in the home. Can identify uses of rocks and soils in the environment.
Rocks can be grouped according to observable characteristics. You can observe and compare rocks.	**2 How are they different?** Children learn to observe differences and similarities between rocks. They learn that rocks can form in many different ways.	Make relevant observations.	Use of descriptive words. Grouping by type. Collect new words from reading	**Task Sheet 2.** CD-ROMs and Internet.	Can name differences between two or more rocks. Can describe similarities.
To model the structure of some rocks in an appealing way.	**3 Make a no-bake rock cake.** Children observe how a mixture of particles can be bound and solidified and compare this to the formation of some rocks.		Read and follow instructions. Measure quantities by weight.	Safety! Check for nut allergies. Melting chocolate needs adult supervision.	Can understand that the cake models the particulate form of many rocks.
To identify differences between rocks by testing	**4 How hard?** Children see that the properties of rocks can be tested. They see that some rocks are much harder than others.	Know that there are different ways of answering scientific questions.	Use of descriptive words. Grouping by type. Collect new words from reading.	Database software.	Know that rocks vary in hardness. Can suggest ways of testing for hardness.
To identify differences between rocks by testing.	**5 Scratch test.** Children classify rocks in order of hardness.	With support, make a general statement about some simple patterns in results.		**Task Sheet 3.** Database software.	Can explain their results in terms of comparative hardness.
To understand that rocks are chosen for particular purposes because of their characteristics.	**6 The rock house.** Children see that rock is used for building materials and that it has many different properties and uses.			**Task Sheet 4.**	Can recognise the reasons for using a number of familiar rocks in house building.
To learn that beneath all surfaces there is rock.	**7 Looking for a soil profile.** Children observe the change in a soil profile with depth and label one soil profile.			**Task Sheet 5.**	Can understand the basic structure of the Earth.
To learn that soil is made up of eroded rock.	**8 Where does soil come from?** Children understand the processes of rock erosion.			Graphics software.	Can explain the origin of soil.
To learn that there are different kinds of soil depending on the rock from which the soil comes.	**9 Different rocks, different soils.** The relationship between rock and soil is reinforced and the components of soil are more clearly investigated using settling experiments.		Use of descriptive words. Grouping by type. Collect new words from reading.	Safety! Children should wear plastic gloves to handle soil.	Can understand that soil is made with rock particles. Can understand that soil and rock are linked.

Learning objective: Knowledge and understanding	Task	Learning objective: Skills	Literacy and numeracy links	Resources and safety	Evidence of learning Children:
To observe differences while handling soil and make comparisons between soil types.	**10 Soil sausages.** Children experience the different properties of soils through handling and carrying out a test to compare various soils.	Make relevant observations. Know that there are different ways of answering scientific questions.		Safety! Children should wear plastic gloves to handle soil.	Can explain their test results in terms of the behaviour of soils.
To learn that particles of different sizes can be separated by sieving.	**11 A problem at the builder's yard.** Children learn that sieving can be used to seperate soils and stones. They learn to select suitable equipment for their separating tests.	In a fair test, identify what to keep the same. With support, plan main steps in an enquiry.		**Task Sheet 6.**	Can select and use sieves to separate particles of different sizes.
To use simple apparatus to measure volumes of liquids and to measure time. To recognise when a test is unfair. To make a graph from results	**12 Which soil drains the fastest?** Children observe and record the different drainage properties of soils through a fair test investigation.	In a fair test, identify what to keep the same. With support, plan main steps in an enquiry.	Measure volume and time, using standard measures. Make a graph from results.	**Task Sheet 7, 8.** Database software. Safety! Children should wear plastic gloves to handle soil.	Can plan a simple test to compare drainage. Can explain their results and relate these to the structure of the soils.
To use their knowledge to solve a practical problem.	**13 Hannah's garden.** Children learn how the properties of soils affect their usage. They see that garden soils can be tested to solve a drainage problem.	With support, plan main steps in an enquiry. Sometimes predict outcomes of an enquiry.	Non-fiction reading and comprehension, including dialogue presented in a story.		Can plan an enquiry to solve a problem. Can predict the outcome of their enquiry.
To plan a fair test. To interpret data. To use the results of an enquiry to make comparisons and draw and explain conclusions.	**14 Hannah's test.** Children learn that the properties of soil can be changed by mixing different kinds of soil together. They plan a test.	Plan a fair test. Interpret data. Use data to make comparisons and draw and explain conclusions.	Interpret data to complete a table and make a graph.	**Task Sheet 8, 9.** Graphing software.	Can explain their results. Can relate their results to the behaviour of different soils.
To plan a fair test and interpret data.	**15 Test how well two soils drain.** Children investigate the drainage efficiency of two different soils.			**Task Sheet 10.**	Can plan an enquiry to solve a problem. Can relate their results to the behaviour of soils.
To provide self-assessment of learning.	**Checkpoint 1.** Children investigate what certain items are made of by investigating labels. **Checkpoint 2.** Children show their understanding of soils and plant growth by answering questions.				
	Summary. Children read through the statements and complete the **Science Log.**			**Science Log.**	
	Assessment Tasks. Children do structured tests to assess their knowledge, skills and understanding of rocks and soils.			**Assessment Task Sheets A and B.**	

TASK 1

Rocks and soils in the kitchen

Purpose

To understand that rocks are used for a variety of everyday purposes.

What to do

Begin by looking around the classroom for things made from the products of rocks and soils. You may have: metal door handles, sink and taps, glass windows, bricks or clay tiles, a china cup or mug, a variety of plastic items, a 'quartz' clock, bricks or breeze blocks may be visible, held together with mortar. You will certainly have chalk!
Discuss with the children how these items are made:

Metals come from rocks called ores.
Glass is made from special sand and limestone, heated together.
Bricks, tiles and chimney pots are made from clay.
Pottery is made from clay.
Plastics are made from oil, which is formed deep under the ground.
Modern clocks contain quartz rock.
Breeze blocks are made from cinders, sand and cement.
Mortar is made from lime, sand, cement and water.
Chalk is a kind of limestone.

Ask the children to complete **Task Sheet 1**, identifying examples of the products of rocks and soils in a typical kitchen.

QUESTIONS

- What is this made from?
- Where is that material found?
- How do we use it?
- Now think about your bathroom at home.
  How many things in there are made with rocks and soils?

Watch out for!

Some of the origins are difficult to follow. How can a new plastic toy be traced back to sticky black oil? The chemistry involved is complex to explain,

ICT OPPORTUNITY

CD-ROMs and Internet sites are a good source of information about materials that originate from rocks.

TASK 2

How are they different?

Purpose

To understand that rocks can be grouped according to observable characteristics.
To show children how to observe and compare rocks.

What to do

Children work with a pair of contrasting rocks. Initially, it is important to use two rocks with distinctive differences. With practice, you can use rocks with more subtle differences and greater similarities. Get the children to record their observations in a table using **Task Sheet 2**.

A rock collection can be bought complete from a supplier or you might collect rocks on holidays and trips. In this case, you may need to have the rocks named by an expert. It is not as important to learn the names of rocks as it is to recognise similarities and differences - but children will want to know them!

Rocks are divided into three groups. **Igneous** - formed from the cooling of hot, molten rock; **sedimentary** - formed when layers of rock were laid down as sediments; and **metamorphic** - sedimentary or igneous rocks changed by pressure and/or heat.

A possible collection could include:

Basalt a dark igneous rock with tiny crystals.
Breccia angular rock fragments stuck together.
Chalk limestone rock made from sea creatures.
Coal the black shiny fossil remains of plants.
Conglomerate pebbles stuck together.
Dolerite dark igneous rock with black or green crystals.
Gneiss banded, stripy metamorphic rock.
Granite igneous rock full of crystals.
Limestone sedimentary rock, often rich in fossils.
Marble sugary metamorphic rock.
Mudstone fine-grained sedimentary rock.
Obsidian black igneous 'glass'.
Pumice the light, solidified froth from lava.
Sandstone grainy sedimentary rock.
Schist silvery metamorphic rock.
Shale sedimentary rock that splits easily.
Slate easily split metamorphic rock.

QUESTIONS

- What can you see?
- Are there particles in the rock?
- Are they big or small?
- What more can you see if you wet the rock?
- What more can you see with a hand lens?
- What other differences do you notice? Shape? Size? Smoothness? Weight?

Watch out for!

Water smoothes the surface of the rock, reflecting light more evenly and making the particles easier to see. Pebbles in streams look more attractive than when they have dried out!

ICT OPPORTUNITY

CD-ROMs and Internet sites are a good source of information on rocks and their origins.

TASK 3 Make a no-bake rock cake

Purpose

To model the structure of some rocks in a way that will appeal to children.

What to do

A recipe for no-bake rock cake is given in the **Pupil's Book**. Melting the chocolate is either an adult task or one to do under close adult supervision. Following the instructions gives you a number of little cakes something like conglomerate or brecchia. It is hard to imagine molten rock - like the chocolate - but children may have seen films of lava flows and could imagine how this might carry away rock particles to bind them together when cool.

QUESTIONS	*Possible answers*
• What is happening to the chocolate?	*It is melting - becoming liquid.*
• Can rocks do this?	*Yes - at very high temperatures.*
• What happens when we add the fruit and biscuit?	*It is bound together by the chocolate.*
• Where have you seen that in the rocks?	*Some rocks are bound together like this.*
• Another name for conglomerate rock is 'pudding stone'. Why do you think that is?	*It binds together rock particles like the fruit in a pudding.*

Watch out for!

Safety! Children should not be allowed to taste the cake if it contains nuts, unless you are confident that they do not suffer from potentially fatal **nut allergies**. Some children – e.g. diabetics – will be unable to eat the finished cake unless special ingredients are used.

TASK 4 How hard?

Purpose

To identify differences in types of rock by simple testing.

What to do

Get the children to rub different rocks together. Hard rocks will scratch softer ones. This fact can be used to order rocks by hardness; but it is important to choose rocks with relatively large differences between them.

You could also try these two related tests:
See which rocks will leave a mark on paper. Put some scrap paper on a board to protect the table and rub the rocks on the paper. Some rocks will leave a mark, others will tear the paper. Try putting drops of water on different rocks with a dropper or a drinking straw. Some rocks are permeable, others are not.

QUESTIONS	*Possible answers*
• Which is your hardest rock? How do you know?	*It will scratch all the other rocks.*
• Which is your softest rock? How do you know?	*It is scratched by all the other rocks.*
• Explain the order you have put your rocks in.	

Watch out for!

Safety! Ensure that children do not rub rock particles into their eyes.

ICT OPPORTUNITY

Children could use a database to store information about the properties of their rocks.

TASK 5

Scratch test

Purpose

To identify differences between rocks through testing.

What to do

Ask the children to try scratching rock samples with a thumbnail (soft) a 2p coin (harder) and a steel nail (hard). This is a version of the tests for Moh's Scale - the internationally recognised hardness test for rocks. Using **Task Sheet 3**, get the children to record their observations in a table, and use the results to rank the rocks in order of hardness. Diamonds are the hardest known rocks. They achieve their strength - and their sparkle – from the bonding of carbon atoms in a very tight lattice structure. The same atoms, bound more loosely, slip from the tip of a graphite pencil when we write, or rub from the surface of charcoal. Diamonds are not indestructible; but they are resistant to extreme heat and pressure.

QUESTIONS

- What scratches this rock?
- Would you call this rock soft or hard?
- Is it softer or harder than that rock?
- Which is your hardest rock?
- How do you know?
- Which is your softest rock?
- How do you know?

Watch out for!

Safety! Ensure that children do not rub rock particles into their eyes.

ICT OPPORTUNITY

Children could use a simple database to classify their rocks.

The rock house

TASK 6

Purpose

To understand that rocks are chosen for particular purposes because of their characteristics and properties.

What to do

Ask the children to read the **Fact File** on page 8. They should then use **Task Sheet 4** to help them identify the materials that are used to make a house. Most of these materials are - or originated as - rocks and soils. Answers include: Sand, limestone and clay for cement and mortar; Clay for roofing tiles - or slate; Clay for bricks and chimney pots; Oil for plastic fittings - pipes, drain pipes and gutters - even some window frames; Metal ores for pipes, sinks, taps, handles; Gypsum for plaster; Sand and limestone for glass and glass fibre.

QUESTIONS

- What is this made from?
- Which of these are rocks?

Watch out for!

Look at local houses to help answer the questions. Expect children to reflect local materials - not necessarily those shown on the picture - in their answers. Remember that regional differences in houses often reflect the local availability of materials.
The connection of oil to plastic is a difficult one to grasp.

Looking for a soil profile

TASK 7

Purpose

To understand that beneath all the Earth's surfaces there is rock.

What to do

It may be possible for you to dig a 'soil profile' somewhere in your school grounds, by shifting a large amount of soil - possibly onto a plastic sheet - and replacing it later. But this may be quite impractical and very time-consuming, and a more efficient approach is to take advantage of someone else's digging! You may have a building site close to the school, or a pipeline or cable being laid, offering you the opportunity to see the layers of soil under the surface. But see the safety note below.

Soils vary, but you can usually see the crumbly topsoil, and recognise roots, showing that this is the layer where plants grow. Further down is the wetter and more compact subsoil, and below that the number of rocks increases. In some cases, the hole may go down as far as the bedrock itself.

Ask the children to look at the soil profile on **Task Sheet 5**, and to label the different layers.

QUESTIONS — *Possible answers*

- What layers can you see?
- What are the names of the different layers?
- Where are the plants growing? — *In the topsoil.*
- What is below the subsoil? — *A rocky layer.*
- What is under the soil layers? — *Bedrock.*

Watch out for!

Safety! This is an excellent opportunity to teach about safety and building sites. Demonstrate by your visit that you take safety seriously and that building sites are not playgrounds.

If you are unable to see a soil profile, use pictures of cliffs, quarries, mountain rock faces and landscapes with rocky outcrops, to demonstrate that there is rock beneath our feet wherever we may be. Challenge the children by asking them what is at the bottom of the sea. Does this mean that there is rock beneath our feet wherever we may be?

TASK 8

Where does soil come from?

Purpose

To learn that soil is formed by the erosion of rock.

What to do

The story of Roger Rock and his transformation to Simon Soil provides a way of explaining that soil is made up of eroded rock.

Watch out for!

Children may find the concept of water knocking off chips of rock difficult to understand.

ICT OPPORTUNITY

Children could use a simple graphics programme to illustrate how rocks become soil.

TASK 9

Different rocks, different soils

Purpose

To learn that there are different kinds of soil depending on the rock from which they come.

What to do

Elicit children's ideas about where soil comes from. The story in Task 8 sets the scene for an understanding of what makes up soil. Shaking or stirring soil samples with water gives a good idea of the different components that make up soils. This can be done in any transparent container, which becomes a 'settling jar'. You can make these by cutting off the bottom halves of large plastic drinks bottles. Some of the plant and animal matter will float on the surface. Fine particles - silts and clays - settle very slowly, clouding the water. Leave overnight to settle out this part. Small particles - like sand, settle after a short time, and pebbles fall immediately to the bottom. This process creates a layered effect in the settling jar, and gives a very good idea of the composition of the soil.

QUESTIONS	*Possible answers*
∘ How many layers can you see in the settling jar?	
∘ What is floating?	*You can often see twigs and leaves.*
∘ What is in the water?	*'Dirt' - actually fine particles of silt and clay.*
∘ What can you see at the bottom?	*Sand and pebbles.*
∘ What differences can you see between the two soils?	*Sandy soil will have thicker bottom layers; clay soils make more 'dirty water'.*

Watch out for!

Safety! Children must wear plastic gloves to handle soils.

TASK 10

Soil sausages

Purpose

To observe differences in the way various soils handle, and to make comparisons between them.

What to do

Encourage the children to try rolling and shaping different damp soils. Clay is a malleable material that can be easily shaped. The fine particles of clay hold water around them, making the clay silky and sticky. Sand is made from larger particles. They don't stick together so well and it is impossible to shape dry sand. Damp sand can be used for castles, but collapses if it dries out. Generally speaking, the more clay in the soil, the better it will form and keep shapes.

QUESTIONS	*Possible answers*
- What shape can you make with that soil?	
- Why do you think those two soils are different?	
- What difference does clay make to that soil?	*The more clay, the easier it is to shape.*
- Here is some sand. How much is it like your soil?	
- Here is some clay. How much is it like your soil?	
- Would you call that a clay soil, or a sandy soil?	

Watch out for!

Safety! Children must wear plastic gloves to handle soils.

TASK 11

A problem at the builder's yard

Purpose

To learn that particles of different sizes can be separated by sieving.

What to do

Ask the children to look at the various stones and sieves on **Task Sheet 6**, and to consider how they would separate the different sizes of stone.

The children should copy and complete the table in the **Pupil's Book**. The key to this exercise is to pick the best sieve to start with (the one that would stop only the largest size of stone). Once this decision is made, the children can progress through the sieves, removing one size of stone on each occasion.

QUESTIONS

- How are you going to separate the stones?
- Which sieve would remove all the large stones?
- Which sieve would let through only the smallest stones?
- Put the sieves in order by size of holes or 'mesh'.

Watch out for!

Extend the exercise with a real separation activity in the classroom. You need not use soils; anything that can be separated with a sieve – seeds, foods, beads etc – are perfect.

TASK 12 Which soil drains the fastest?

Purpose

To extend children's understanding of the characteristics of sandy soil, clay and loam. To use simple apparatus to measure volumes of liquids and to measure time. To recognise when a test is unfair.

What to do

Provide three different soils for children to plan and carry out an investigation to find out which soil drains the fastest. For the sake of simplicity, you could provide sand and moulding clay as two of the soils, as well as a soil sample. Children use the planning board on **Task Sheet 7** to help them organize the investigation and report the results. You could, however, do one experiment for the whole class.

Set up three funnels, each full of one of the soils. The samples could be called clay, sand and loam. The clay should fill the funnel completely. If you set a lump of clay inside the funnel, the water will not drain through it, but simply run round it. Sand should be held back by paper, or it will all run through. For fairness, the other soils should be treated in the same way. The test would also be unfair if the amounts of soil and water were different, or the apparatus used made great differences in the experimental conditions.

Pour the water through the samples simultaneously and measure how much has drained through each one after 3 minutes. Compare the time it takes for the water to drain completely. Children should discover that the clay took longest and held the most water. Using computer software or **Task Sheet 8**, get the children to use the results to make a graph.

Watch out for!

Safety! Children must wear plastic gloves to handle soils.

ICT OPPORTUNITY

Children could use a database to store their soil data and create a graph using computer software.

TASK 13 Hannah's garden

Purpose

To reinforce and extend children's understanding of different soil types. To plan a fair test.

What to do

Tasks 13, 14, 15 form an extended enquiry, placed in the context of a garden and gardener. They build on the facts established in Task 12, but, with support, could be done as a stand-alone activity. Hannah finds by investigation and from a secondary source that the soil at the back of her house is clay. She adds sand to it, making it loam.

TASK 14

Hannah's test

Purpose

To apply knowledge of soil types to solving a practical problem. To make and record measurements of time and volume of water. To use the results to make comparisons and draw and explain conclusions.

What to do

Get the children to suggest how Hannah could investigate two different soils. Use the planning board on **Task Sheet 9** to plan a test. To make the test fair, the size of the soil sample and the amount of water used must stay the same.

Hannah starts by making direct observations. How does the soil feel; how well does it shape? Then she looks at its drainage. She could measure one or both of two things – how much water drains through each soil, and how long water takes to drain through the soil.

Get the children to plot Hannah's results on a simple bar chart in which the soil types (front and back gardens) are on the x-axis, and the results - in millilitres or seconds – are up the y-axis. This is a good opportunity to use computer software, or the children could use the standard graph on **Task Sheet 8**. Encourage them to tell the story of the graph. They might do this in the form of a letter to Hannah.

QUESTIONS

- Which soil do you predict will hold the most water?
- Which soil do you predict will take the longest to drain?
- How could you measure the time each sample takes?
- How are you going to record your results?
- What will your table look like?
- What sort of graph could you draw?
- What will you put on the x-axis?
- What will you put on the y-axis?
- What can Hannah learn from your graph?
- What can Hannah do to improve her garden?

Watch out for!

In practice, gardeners add lime to heavy clay soils. The lime causes the clay to **flocculate** – the tiny particles cling together – and so the soil is lightened.

ICT OPPORTUNITY

Children could create a graph of their results using computer software.

TASK 15 Test how well two soils drain

Purpose

To plan a fair test. To set up an investigation into how well soils drain.

What to do

Provide two different soils for children to plan how well soils drain, i.e. how much of the water that is poured in comes out. The experiment should be set up like that in Task 12 but soil samples could be more like each other. Make sure that enough time is given to allow the water to flow through the soil completely. Children can use the planning board on **Task Sheet 10** and refer to Hannah's test in Task 14 to help them with their answers.

Watch out for!

Safety! Children must wear plastic gloves to handle soils.

CHECKPOINT 1 The rock inspector

Encourage children to investigate what things such as pumice, talcum powder and toothpaste are made of by reading labels, or looking up these words in a dictionary or encyclopedia. Some of this information will be available on CD-ROMs or on the Internet.

CHECKPOINT 2 Wonder Soil

Prompt reactions from the class with questions such as:

- Will holding lots of water make the soil better or worse for most plants?
- Will having no air be good for the plants or not?
- Will having no air mean that you could grow more plants?

S Summary

An opportunity for the children to assess their own progress using the **Science Log**. Tell the children to circle the face that best reflects how confident they are with each statement.

Assessment Tasks

A

An assessment of children's learning. Give the children **Assessment Task Sheets A** and **B**
The questions are below, with selected answers in *italics*.

ANSWERS

1

Slate is like this	This makes slate good for roofs because
Slate is waterproof	*It keeps rain and snow out.*
Slate splits into large flat sheets	*It can be put on the roof like tiles.*
You can drill holes through slate	*You can nail slates to the roof timbers.*
Slate can be cut into shapes	*You can cut slates for the roof.*

2 Jenny and Chris were on a boat. They were in the middle of the sea.
"If you fell in the sea now, you would sink down for ever,"said Jenny.
"I don't think that's right,"said Chris.
Who was right? Why? *Chris was right. At the bottom of the sea there are rocks, as there are all over the Earth. Beneath all surfaces there is rock.*

3 Charles Darwin, the famous scientist, found that the worms in his garden turned the soil to loam by their digging.
He found that the worm tunnels helped the water drain away.
He told people that worms were good for the garden.
Was he right? Why? *The worms broke up the soil to loam. Loam is a good soil for growing plants. The worm tunnels added to the drainage so that the soil did not become waterlogged.*

B

1 Rajan found his brother picking up sugar cubes one by one.
"What are you doing?" he asked.
"The granulated sugar got in with the cubes by mistake. So I am separating them."
"There's an easier way than that," said Rajan.
What was Rajan's easy way? *Rajan could use a sieve. If he put the cubes and granulated sugar in a sieve and shook it, the granulated sugar would pass through and the sugar cubes would be held back.*

2 Mr. and Mrs. Powell were looking round a brand new house.
Mr. Powell was unhappy. "Look at this," he said.
He squeezed soil from the garden in his hand. "They've taken all the topsoil away. We're left with clay." How did Mr. Powell know what had happened? What could Mr. and Mrs. Powell do about the clay? *Mr. Powell tried squeezing the soil. He found that it made a shape - a sign that there was a lot of clay there. Topsoil doesn't shape like this. It is common practice to remove topsoil from building sites before building. If it is not put back, it can take many years before the soil is fertile and draining well. Mr. and Mrs. Powell could add sand to improve the soil, or cover the clay with topsoil.*

Task Sheet 1

Name .... *Date* ....

Write and draw lines to show which parts of the kitchen are made from rocks and soils. Try to say which kinds of rocks or soils they are made from.

Task Sheet 2

Name .... *Date* ....

Use this sheet to record the differences between your two rocks.
Record as many differences as you can find.

My first rock	My second rock

Now look closely at your rocks with a magnifying glass. It may help to wet the surface of each rock. Draw here what you see:

Task Sheet 3

Name .... *Date* ....

Try to scratch each rock with your thumbnail. Put a tick in the box if you can. Put a cross in the box if you can't.

Now try again with a 2p coin.
Now try again with a steel nail.

Rock	**Thumb nail**	**2p coin**	**Steel nail**

Now put the rocks in order, starting with the softest. Some rocks may belong in the same box.

Softest rock			**Hardest rock**

Can you find a way to test the rocks again so that there is only one rock in each column?

Task Sheet 4

Name .... *Date* ....

Many parts of this house are made from rocks and soils.
Label the parts of the house with the material they are made from.

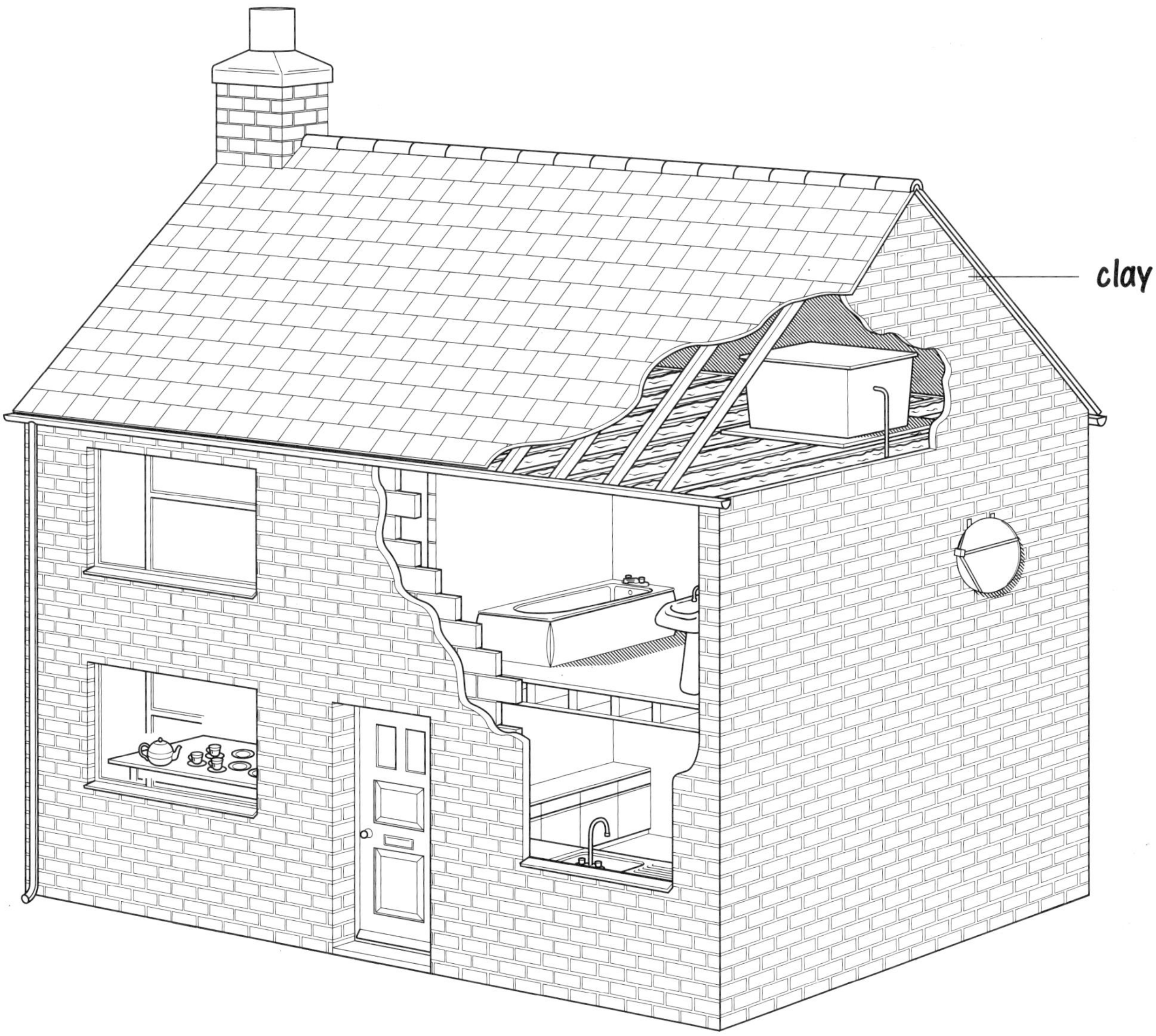

Task Sheet 5

Name .... *Date* ....

Draw lines to join the words to the correct place on the soil profile.

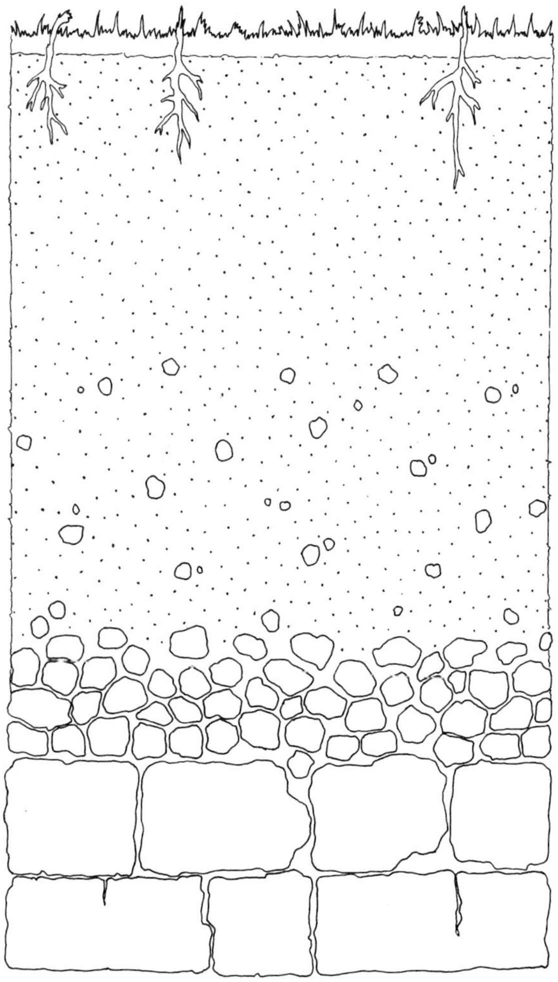

Bedrock

Topsoil

Rocky soil

Subsoil

Where do the plants grow? Explain why.

____

____

____

Task Sheet 6

Name .... *Date* ....

Which sieve will Sally need for the gravel?

Tick the stones that will fall through.

Sieve A	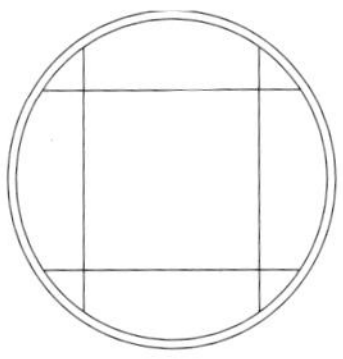	large stone ☐	medium stone ☐	small stone ☐	gravel ☐
Sieve B	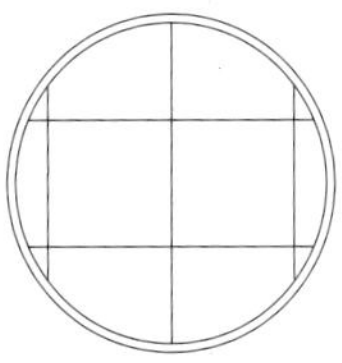	large stone ☐	medium stone ☐	small stone ☐	gravel ☐
Sieve C	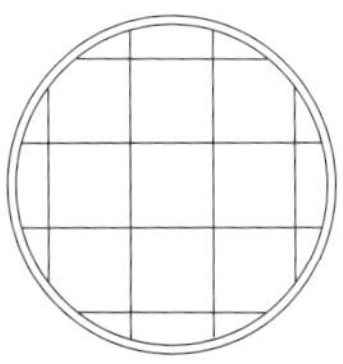	large stone ☐	medium stone ☐	small stone ☐	gravel ☐
Sieve D	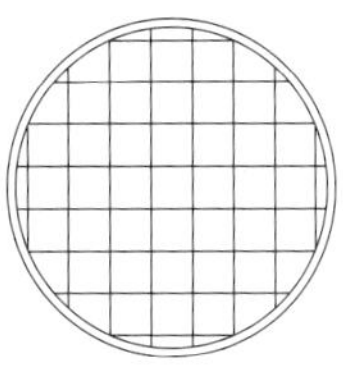	large stone ☐	medium stone ☐	small stone ☐	gravel ☐
Sieve E	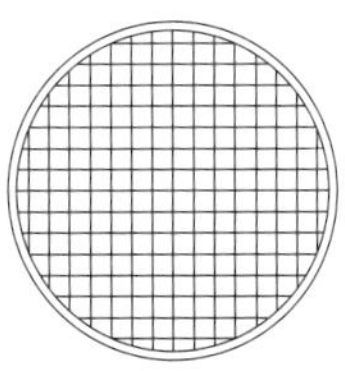	large stone ☐	medium stone ☐	small stone ☐	gravel ☐

Task Sheet 7

Name .... *Date* ....

Our question:

We will change:

We will measure:

We will keep these things the same to make our test fair:

This is the table we will use to record our results.

Soil	Time left to drain	Amount of water that drained through

We will make a graph from our results.

Task Sheet 8

Name .... *Date* ....

When you draw your graph, remember to think about:
Leaving space between the bars, the scale, labels for each axis and a title for the graph.

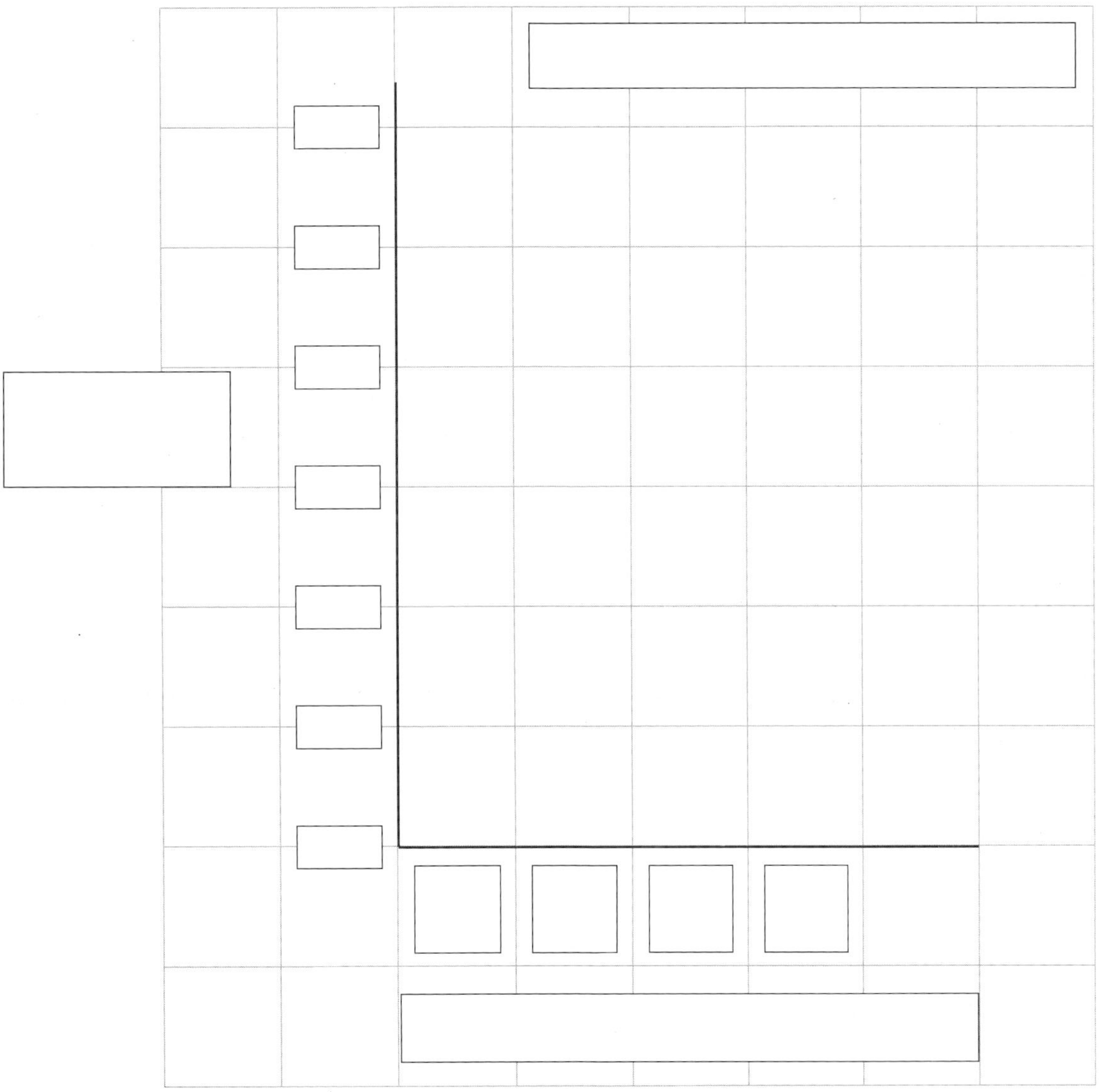

We think our graph tells us that:

___

___

Task Sheet 9

Name .... *Date* ....

Hannah wanted to find out more about her two soils. She decided to compare how they drained. This is her investigation plan. Finish it for her.

I am going to investigate ______________________________

I am going to measure ______________________________

or I might measure ______________________________

To make my test fair, I must keep these the same:

____

____

____

____

Here is what Hannah found. Record her results in the table?

I found that my front garden soil was gritty and rough. When I added 250 ml of water to it, 200 ml drained through in 3 minutes, and it made good sausage shapes.

I found that my back garden soil drained really slowly (7 minutes) with the same amount of water, and it held back 130 ml. It makes great shapes because it is so smooth and sticky.

	Front garden soil	**Back garden soil**
How does it feel?		
How does it shape?		
How much water did I add to it?		
How much water drained through?		
How long did it take until the water stopped draining?		

Task Sheet 10

Name .... *Date* ....

Our question:

____

We will change:

____

We will measure:

____

We will keep these things the same to make our test fair:

____

Science Log

Name .... *Date* ....

- I know that you can use rocks for many different purposes.
- I know that you can sort rocks by how they look.
- I know that different rocks suit different jobs.
- I know that there is rock under you, wherever you are.
- I know that different types of rock make different types of soil.
- I know that you can separate particles of different sizes by sieving.
- I can find differences between rocks by testing.
- I can observe and compare rocks.
- I can observe differences between soils and make comparisons.
- I can measure amounts of liquids and time.
- I can plan a fair test.

Assessment Task Sheet A

Name .... Date ....

1 Many old houses have slate roofs. Sheets of slate are nailed to the top of the house. Slate is a special rock. Fill in the spaces on this table to say why slate makes good roofs:

Slate is like this	This makes slate good for roofs because
Slate is waterproof	
Slate splits into large flat sheets	
You can drill holes through slate	
Slate can be cut into shapes	

2 Jenny and Chris were on a boat. They were in the middle of the sea. "If you fell in the sea now you would sink down forever," said Jenny. "I don't think that's right," said Chris. Who was right? Why?

____

____

____

3 Charles Darwin, the famous scientist, found that the worms in his garden turned the soil to loam by their digging.
He found that the worm tunnels helped the water drain away.
He told people that worms were good for the garden. Was he right? Why?

____

____

____

Assessment Task Sheet B

Name .... *Date* ....

1 Rajan found his brother picking up sugar cubes one by one.
"What are you doing?" he asked.
"The granulated sugar got in with the cubes by mistake.
So I am separating them."
"There's an easier way than that," said Rajan.
What was Rajan's easy way?

____

____

____

2 Mr. and Mrs. Powell were looking round a brand new house.
Mr. Powell was unhappy. "Look at this," he said. He squeezed soil from the garden in his hand. "They've taken all the topsoil away. We're left with clay."
How did Mr. Powell know what had happened?
What could Mr. and Mrs. Powell do about the clay?

____

____

____

Curriculum Links

England and Wales National Curriculum

Sc1 Scientific enquiry – 1a, 1b, 2a, 2b, 2c, 2d, 2e, 2f, 2h, 2i, 2j, 2k, 2l, 2m

Sc3 Materials and their properties – 1a, 1d, 3a

Northern Ireland Curriculum

Key Stage 2 Materials:

Properties (a, b, c)

Change (e)

Environmental Studies 5-14: Science

Earth and Space:

On planet Earth – level D

Materials from Earth – level E (give further examples of the links between the properties of materials and their uses)

NEW STAR SCIENCE SKILLS LADDER

	Planning					Obtaining and presenting evidence			Considering evidence and evaluating			
	Asking questions and having ideas	**Deciding an appropriate approach**	**Planning the detail of what to do**	**Predicting what might happen**	**Choosing what equipment to use**	**Using equipment and carrying out practical work safely**	**Making observations and taking measurements**	**Presenting evidence**	**Drawing conclusions and describing patterns and trends**	**Comparing results to predictions and making further predictions**	**Explaining evidence**	**Evaluating**
Year 2	With support, asks questions leading to scientific enquiry.	Sorts questions into those that can be answered by trying it out and those that cannot.	With support, describes the observations or measurements they need to take, spots when a plan will lead to an unfair test and recognises hazards.	With support, sometimes predicts outcomes of enquiries.	Chooses appropriate equipment from a limited range with support from the teacher.	Follows instructions for using equipment correctly and safely, usually working without adult support.	Makes relevant observations. Takes non-standard measurements. Begins to use basic equipment for measuring quantities such as length or mass, in standard units.	Uses drawings and labels to present evidence. Uses prepared tables and bar charts.	Describes what happened, making comparisons where appropriate. With support, orders results where appropriate.	Says whether what happened was expected. With support, makes further predictions from results in simple contexts.	Recognises cause and effect in most simple situations.	Recognises some of the difficulties encountered. With support, suggests how these might be avoided.
Year 3	Sometimes asks questions leading to scientific enquiry.	Knows there are different ways of answering scientific questions.	In a fair test, identifies what to keep the same. With support plans main steps in other types of enquiry. Recognises most hazards.	Sometimes predicts outcomes to enquiries.	Selects appropriate equipment from a wider range with support from the teacher.	Uses basic equipment correctly and safely. Usually refers to adult when equipment fails.	Makes relevant observations. Uses standard measuring equipment for quantities such as temperature and volume.	Sometimes creates own tables and bar charts.	With support, makes a general statement about some simple patterns in results.	With support, makes further predictions from results in simple contexts.	With support, provides explanations for simple patterns in results.	Recognises the difficulties encountered. With support suggests how the enquiry might be improved.
Year 4	Asks questions and offers own ideas for scientific enquiry.	With support knows when to answer a question by using a fair test and when evidence should be collected in other ways.	In a fair test, identifies what to keep the same and with support what to change and what to measure/observe. Plans main steps in other enquiries. Recognises hazards and support, plans how to control risks.	Predicts outcomes and sometimes suggests reasons for their prediction.	Selects appropriate equipment and with support, considers the scale and the degree of accuracy required on some measuring equipment.	Uses basic equipment correctly and safely. Begins to deal with equipment failures.	Makes a series of observations. Uses standard measuring equipment for measuring most quantities.	Creates own tables and bar charts. Uses a line chart with support.	Makes a general statement about simple patterns in results.	Makes further predictions from results in simple contexts.	Provides explanations for simple patterns in results.	Suggests how the enquiry might be improved. With support, recognises some of the limitations of their evidence.